007835

Designed for beginning student and amateur, this new series shows how to create attractive items with inexpensive materials and a minimum of equipment. In each, one fascinating craft is simplified and exact directions are given for a wide variety of articles. The author, Jutta Lammer, is a noted German art educator and craftsman.

MAKE YOUR OWN COSTUME JEWELRY
MAKE YOUR OWN GIFTS
MAKE THINGS WITH STRAW AND RAFFIA
PRINT YOUR OWN FABRICS

These **Watson-Guptill Hobby Books**
are now available to schools and libraries in
GOLDENCRAFT BINDING
from GOLDEN PRESS, INC. Educational Division
and its regular distributors.
850 Third Ave., New York, N.Y. 10022

DISCARD

Print Your Own Fabrics

Published MCMLXV by Watson-Guptill Publications, New York, New York

Library of Congress Catalog Card Number 65-21694

Made and printed in The Netherlands

by The Ysel Press, Deventer

Jutta Lammèr

Print Your Own Fabrics

Watson-Guptill Publications

New York

Contents

Fabric printing

The process is a simple one: a printing block made of one or other of the materials listed below is covered with dye and pressed on to the fabric. This method of decorating textiles differs essentially from batik, where the fabric is immersed in a dye bath, often successively in different colours, and from fabric painting, in which the work is done with a brush. It therefore produces quite different results.

Printing blocks can be cut from potatoes, turnips, corks, rubber, wood and linoleum; potatoes and linoleum are most generally used. A potato can only be employed to make a 'positive' block—that is, one in which the design stands out in relief—but linoleum allows 'negative' cutting as well. In a positive block, which is more difficult to produce than a negative one, but easier to print from, the shape of the pattern appears in colour on the fabric and the intervening spaces remain clear. The negative block prints the spaces between the patterns and the pattern shapes are left uncoloured.

When printing on fabrics the finished impression should always typify the material of which the block is made; there should be no attempt to make a potato print look like a lino print, or *vice versa*. Hand printing on fabrics must be neat, but not too mechanically accurate. Never aim at absolute perfection, or take machine-printed fabrics as your model.

Potato blocks

Potato blocks are extremely easy to make, but they do not last long. By the end of a day they will have shrunk, and the outlines will have altered so much that they can no longer be used. A further disadvantage of the potato block is that only relatively small motifs can be printed from it. Its chief use is for composing varied patterns by a rhythmical repetition of formal elements alongside, above and below one another. Even a single

Equipment for printing
from a potato block

Cut a large potato in half

Cut out a simple motif in relief

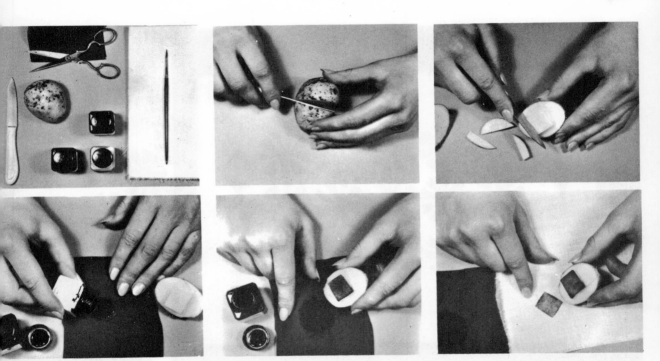

Liquid fabric-painting ink
is poured on to an improvised
printing pad lying on
a glass sheet

The block is pressed down
on the pad

Imprint of the potato block
on the fabric

block in the form of a triangle or square can produce very decorative results.

Moreover, printing with potato blocks is a technique which even children can employ successfully, under proper supervision and guidance.

Cutting a block

Having cut a large, well-shaped potato in half, you can carve a simple shape on one of the cut surfaces with either a penknife or a kitchen knife. Work free-hand, without pencilling the outline; the little irregularities are part of the charm of this kind of printing. It is best to start with a square or round form, which can be enriched by notching the edges or varying it in some other way. Thin lines should be avoided because they are liable to break down under the pressure of printing. No curlicues or complicated shapes can be cut in this medium, as you will soon discover for yourself.

After cutting out the pattern, stand the potato for a few minutes on a dry cloth, which will absorb most of the moisture in it. The print will be much clearer if made from a dry block.

Other requisites

Besides the potato block and the fabric to be printed you will need some pieces of non-fraying material fastened together to serve as a printing pad, and a sheet of glass or piece of plastic to lay beneath it, plus your dyes. Although it is really a printing technique that we are concerned with, when using a potato block it is better to choose the more liquid fabric-*painting* inks for the purpose, rather than the somewhat pasty fabric-*printing* inks employed in lino printing.

Choice of fabric

Although almost any smooth fabric free from dressing is suitable for printing on, it is better not to choose anything too coarse, since the texture prevents the relatively small motifs from showing up clearly, and the impression bears a wrong proportion to the material. Cambric, cotton, silk, artificial silk, and linen mixtures are all suitable, and so are fabrics made of synthetic fibres. Coarse linen, jute and loosely woven fabrics should not be used.

Printing

Pour a little of the fabric-painting ink (permanent dye) out of the bottle on to the printing pad and allow it time to sink in. Then press the block carefully, but not too hard, on to the pad, to take up the colour. Take a trial impression from it on a spare piece of the material to be printed. As a rule, several of these tests must be made to find out how hard to press the block on the pad and how to place it on the material to get a clear impression.

After a few tests you can start printing, re-colouring the block for each impression by pressing it on the pad. If the impression is incomplete, the outlines can be filled in later with a paintbrush dipped in the ink. Never attempt to improve a defective impression by setting the block twice over in the same place. This is hardly ever successful, and you will be annoyed with yourself for having tried it.

When printing a large area with a repeated combination of motifs from the same block, it will help you to place them in the right position if you make guide lines—not drawn on the material but simply marked with an iron before beginning to print. This is easy to do, and will provide you with useful points of reference.

If a pattern of different motifs is to be repeated over a large surface, it is best to print all the motifs of one kind first, thus giving a pleasant distribution of space, and then to fit in the others. See, for example, the white

Simple flower patterns like this look particularly well on tablecloths and mats. They are also suitable for greeting cards

cambric tablecloth and napkin (p. 13) with red tulips, green stalks and green leaves, printed from three blocks. The red flowers were first distributed over the whole area, then the stalks and then the leaves.

A special effect can be obtained by printing twice with the same block—contrary to the usual method—without giving it a fresh coat of colour. In the illustration with the tulips, the green of the leaves was thus varied in depth.

The same potato block can be used to print in different colours if it is thoroughly washed in clean water and put to dry on a cloth between printings. It is as well to pare a thin slice off it at the same time. It is better, however, not to experiment with too many colours to begin with, but to find things out for yourself in the course of simple work. Once you are sure of being able to set the block down in the right place, and have acquired a reliable sense of space, you can not only carry out complicated

printing schemes, but you will be able to combine two methods: potato-block printing and fabric painting.

Finishing

Materials printed with fabric-painting ink, once the dye has dried in, merely need ironing on the wrong side. The dye is then firmly combined with the weave and will prove both wash- and sun-proof, and proof against boiling and exposure to the weather.

Summary

Important points for the advanced fabric printer to remember:

Application. Potato blocks can always be used for printing small motifs. Materials printed from potato blocks are suitable for tablecloths, table mats and napkins, for curtains and cushion covers, aprons and children's clothes. Potato blocks can also be used for printing personal greeting cards and notepaper.

Tablecloth and napkin of cambric, printed with three different block motifs (flowers, stalks and leaves)

Equipment. A large potato, as free from defects as possible, a penknife or kitchen knife, layers of material to make a printing pad, and a suitable support for it, fabric-painting inks and a paintbrush for corrections.

Fabrics. Silk, artificial silk, cotton, linen mixtures, cambric and synthetic fabrics are all suitable. Jute, open-work materials and coarse weaves must be avoided. All fabrics must be free from dressing (stiffeners or fillers) or have it removed.

Procedure. Cut a simple motif on the half-potato. Pour some dye on the printing pad and allow it to soak in. Then press the potato block upon it, but not too hard. Make a test print on a scrap of the fabric, and then carry out the actual printing. Let the dye become thoroughly dry and then iron the fabric on the wrong side.

Printing from lino blocks

Practice with potato-block printing is of little use when adopting lino blocks, for these entail a much more complicated procedure. Besides being made of entirely different material, lino blocks have not only to be cut with different tools but are larger and require different handling. Even the dye used for printing with them is of a different type from either fabric-painting ink or batik dye, so we must start all over again.

Equipment

For lino-block printing you will need waste pieces of linoleum about ¼ inch thick, obtainable from hobby shops, carpet shops and timber warehouses or lumber yards. Then linoleum cutters of various shapes: at least one sharp-pointed knife-type cutter for fine lines, one V-shaped cutter for medium lines and one U-shaped tool, or gouge, for cutting out and removing larger areas. These cutters are set in handles rather like penholders. You can even improvise a handle by pulling out the metal parts of an ordinary penholder with pincers and pushing the blade of the knife into the opening, wedging it with a little wooden peg to prevent it from slipping out. You will also need a rubber roller and a piece of glass or plastic on which to roll out the ink, and some good quality fabric-printing inks.

Complete sets of this equipment can be bought, but will soon be found inadequate for more than your first attempts, and the best thing is to invest in a set by way of basic equipment, and buy further tools and inks as you go on. Cheap cutting tools soon become blunt and useless, so quality rather than price should be considered.

Choice of design

As usual, the basic rule for the beginner is to be simple and clear.

Curtain with repeat pattern. Two different motifs (positive blocks) are printed alternately and continuously in two colours

In any case the technical difficulties of cutting linoleum require simplification. When working out a design for lino printing, always remember that the print will appear the other way round, mirror fashion. Don't make a plastic design on the paper and try to reproduce it on the block; this will only lead to disappointment. The object in printing a fabric is not to decorate it with a little picture: the main thing is to apportion the space at your command in a significant way. Ornaments are very suitable for the purpose, if only for the number of ways in which they can be combined. Nature also offers a great choice of subjects which can easily be simplified and stylised by restricting yourself to the essential lines and areas needed to make the motif recognisable. All distracting non-essentials should be avoided. A forcibly stylised representation of plants or animals is far more attractive and decorative than a muddled or too detailed design, quite apart from

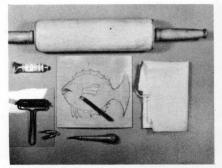

Colouring the block

The design, once traced, or drawn direct, on the lino block, is cut out with a V-tool

Fabric-printing ink is squeezed on to the glass plate . . .

. . . and distributed evenly with the rubber roller

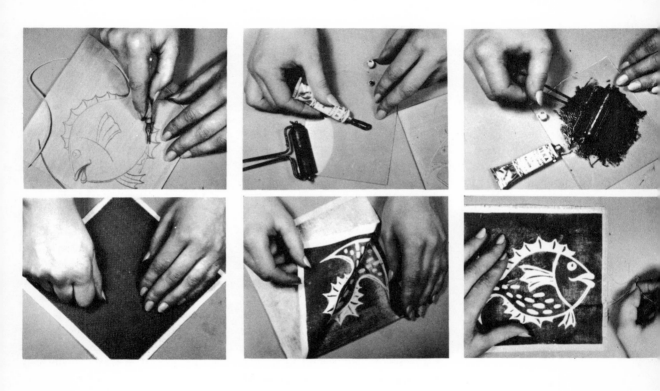

The lino block coated with ink, is laid on the fabric and pressed

After pressing, block and fabric are turned over and the fabric is quickly pulled off the block

The printed fabric is fringed out at the edges

the fact that a simple block is easier to cut and therefore sharper and neater in appearance.

The motif should be neither too small nor too large. Small motifs are more easily and simply printed from potato blocks. Designs that are too large, on the other hand, usually produce uneven prints, especially with negative blocks. They often look heavy, and the fabric becomes rather stiff because of the thick layer of dye.

Positive or negative block?

This question is not easy to answer, because each kind has its charm, but also its advantages and disadvantages. A negative block must, above all, not be too big, or it will look flat. The design stands out as light lines from the coloured ground of the fabric. All the rest of the block appears as a coloured surface, and if its area is too large the imprint will be uneven. The lino cut in the pictures showing the separate stages of the work (pp. 16-17)

is a negative block. All the outlines of the fish motif are cut out of the linoleum and the spaces are left standing. Blocks of this kind are useful for printing little wall hangings, table mats, napkins and other small pieces of fabric. For continuous printing (repeats) on a larger area they are not particularly suitable; positive blocks are better.

Making a positive block takes time and skill, since large areas will have to be removed from some parts of the design if it is to stand out clearly, and it is only too easy to break something down which ought to have been left standing: a further reason for keeping to simple forms. On the whole, positive blocks produce better imprints than negative ones, but with practice you can master both methods equally well.

Transferring the drawing

When you have worked out your motif in its final form, the drawing must be transferred to the lino block, which should be only a little larger than the motif.

There are two ways of doing this. If the drawing allowed for the imprint to appear reversed (mirror fashion), it can be transferred to the linoleum, right side up, by tracing it through a sheet of carbon paper; but if you forgot this, you must lay a piece of carbon paper under the drawing, black side up, and redraw the lines, so that they will be visible on both sides. Now turn the drawing over and lay a piece of carbon paper, black side down, between it and the block, and go over the drawing again. It is advisable to fasten all four sides of the drawing, carbon paper and linoleum together with adhesive strips, so that none of them can get out of position. The drawing transferred to the block should be compared with the original and any necessary corrections made, and then it should be redrawn in Indian ink, to make it easier to work on. When you have acquired a certain amount of practice in cutting, you can omit all this preparation. Many people find that in time they can draw their design straight on to the block, but beginners should not be so bold.

Cutting a negative block

The chief tools to use for cutting a negative block are the knife-type cutter (for the outlines) and a V-tool for cutting and removing lines and small spaces. Hold the handle of the cutting knife like the handle of an ordinary knife and begin cutting a line at the lower edge nearest you, pressing the tool lightly into the linoleum and pushing it slowly forwards. Always work away from yourself, so as not to get hurt if the tool slips. Your left hand, which is holding the block steady, must therefore never be opposite the direction of the cut. It is best to make your first attempt on a spare piece of linoleum. The knife should be pushed forward without too much pressure.

Begin by printing simple forms like these

Appearance of a positive block—
everything that stands out in relief
will show in colour on the fabric

When all the lines have been cleanly
cut out, the negative block is ready
for printing. To get an approximate
idea of its effect, the block can be
damped with water and pressed down
on a piece of paper. This gives you a
chance to make a few slight alterations if you wish to.

Cutting a positive block

The work is not essentially different
from that on a negative block, only
you must think round the other way.
All the outlines of the pattern must
be left standing, and the spaces in
between removed. The upstanding
lines and surfaces of which the block
will eventually consist must not be

too small or weak, because they would
not leave a satisfactory imprint, and
might easily be broken off, ruining
the block. The parts to be left standing are first outlined with the cutting
knife, to establish a definite limit to
the clearing of the background and
prevent awkward mistakes in the
cutting. When the pattern has been
roughly cut out, using the U-shaped
gouge most of the time, you can start
on the finer work. All the outlines
must be gone over again with the V-
tool or the knife, to ensure the ulti-
mate sharpness of the print. The
edges of the block especially must be
cleared of all superfluous linoleum,
to prevent them from printing on the
fabric—a thing that happens more

easily than you might expect. Care must also be taken to ensure that the linoleum between the outlines of the pattern is cleared out sufficiently to prevent it from printing in the intervening spaces. Here too a trial print with water on paper is a help.

Choice of fabric
As in all textile techniques, the fabrics must be free from dressing (stiffeners or fillers). If there is any dressing in them the fabrics must be boiled, or washed in hot soapy water. If the dressing is left in, there is a risk that parts of the printed pattern may be carried away with it in the first wash, because the dye has not been able to combine properly with the weave in some places, but has only adhered to the dressing, which gets dissolved in the wash.

All medium-fine fabrics are suitable for lino-block printing (especially linen mixtures). Soft fabrics like chiffon and silk are not so good, because the dye makes them much heavier and less supple. Fluffy fabrics and those with a nap are no use for printing on. Printed fabrics can be used for a wide range of things, from small tablemats to scarves and table-cloths and even window-blinds and curtains. You can give your printed fabrics a modern touch or not, as you choose.

Preparing to print
Before printing from your lino block, be sure to remove any traces of grease it may have acquired, by washing it in soapy water and letting it dry. Meanwhile, make a printing pad or underlay out of some newspapers, keeping it rather soft, and have some pure turpentine ready in case you need to thin the printing ink, as well as turpentine substitute for cleaning the block. You will also need some old rags for wiping your tools and your hands, a sheet of glass for rolling out the ink and a knife for spreading the ink on it. You can do your printing either on a clean kitchen table or on the floor. The fabric to be printed must be quite smooth, and it is best to iron it before starting work.

Printing
Fabric-printing inks can usually be used straight out of the tube, but if they are too thick they can be slightly thinned with a few drops of pure turpentine (not substitute). They must, however, remain pasty, and on

If the block is wider than the
roller you must work very quickly,
otherwise the ink on the first
half of it will begin to dry

no account be too thin, because this causes blurred prints.

Squeeze out an inch or so from the tube on to the glass or plastic slab and spread it evenly with the knife.

The ink must be rolled out thinly until the roller is entirely coated with it. Now colour the block by running the roller over it several times to and fro. The fabric, previously ironed, must lie ready on the newspaper underlay.

First, however, make a test print on paper, to be sure the ink has been evenly distributed over the block, whether it has the right consistency, and whether the block itself is satisfactory. If not, it will still be possible to make a few slight corrections. If you want to do so, clean the ink off the block with turpentine substitute and make the corrections with a cutting tool.

If the print on the paper shows that the ink has run into the grooves on the block, the ink was too thin. If after rubbing the paper evenly on the block, the print is too faint, the ink was either rolled on too thinly or it was too solid. Do not start printing the fabric till you have obtained a satisfactory print on paper.

Carefully coat the block again with ink with the roller and lay the block quickly on the fabric, taking care not to shift it. To get an even pressure, run a rolling-pin to and fro over the back of the block, or lay a piece of wood on it and give it even, vertical blows with a hammer. The safest way of all, however, to obtain a good print is to work on the floor and simply stand on the block. But whichever method you adopt, you must be sure not to shift the block.

Once the printing is done, block and fabric must be separated. This can be done in two ways: either hold the fabric steady by a projecting corner and lift the block off it quickly, or turn block and fabric upside down and peel the fabric off, beginning at one corner. Both methods give good results.

If the motif is to be repeated on the same piece of fabric, the block must be coated afresh each time with the roller, taking care to keep the layer as much as possible of the same thickness—not too thick and not too thin. After printing, the fabric must be left to dry for a few days. After four weeks the dye will be so fast that the fabric can be washed. All printing tools, block, roller and glass, must be thoroughly cleaned with turpentine substitute. The clean lino block can be stored away and used again any number of times.

Further uses of the block

Lino blocks can be used to print in different colours, either alongside or over one another. You can even print only part of a block and obtain quite a different result.

Printing the motifs side by side in different colours merely necessitates cleaning the block thoroughly with turpentine substitute at each change of colour, as well as the roller and the glass cleaning; the same procedure is necessary when printing one colour over another. Not many blocks, how-ever, will prove suitable for over-printing. It is better to use several motifs with simple basic shapes, and to start printing with the lightest col-our, ending up with the darkest. For instance, you might print a round shape in yellow, then a red star over it, and finally black rays over the star. You can also print a three-pointed star in three different colours, with the points placed intermediately, so that a nine-pointed star results. But the next printing must not be done until the earlier one is dry (about a week), which is unfortunately rather a waste of time.

A partial print can be made by cover-ing the unwanted part with paper before applying the block to the fabric, so that the block prints that part on the paper instead of on the

The two motifs which appeared on p. 15, grouped round a positive print of a horse

Pleasing effects can be
obtained with a single block,
used here to make borders on
a lampshade of a linen mixture

Three negative prints
on the pocket of an apron

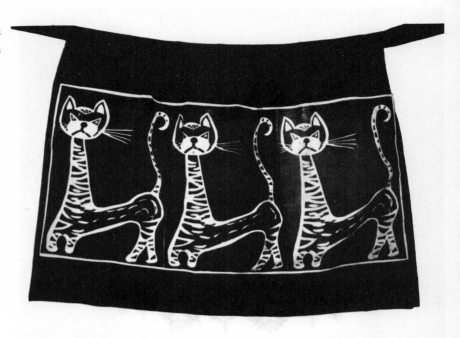

fabric. A continuous print made alternately from blocks and half-blocks can be very attractive if neatly carried out.

Summary
Once you are thoroughly grounded in the essentials of lino printing, you can work along these lines:
Equipment. Linoleum, fabric-printing inks, rubber roller, piece of glass, lino cutters, plus turpentine, turpentine substitute, rags, newspapers for an underlay, and either a rolling-pin or a piece of wood and a hammer.
Fabrics. Medium to coarse weaves, without dressing. Not recommended: silk and all other soft fabrics which lose their plasticity with the concentrated burden of dye.
Kinds of block. Negative blocks produ-

ce coloured surfaces and light lines standing out in the colour of the fabric. Positive blocks print the pattern, leaving everything else untouched, all the surrounding linoleum having been removed.

Making the block. Draw a simple motif on paper in the reverse direction and transfer it to the linoleum by means of carbon paper, redrawing the lines in Indian ink if necessary. Then cut out lines, or outlines of pattern, according to the kind of block, with various cutting tools. Remove any grease from the block by washing it in soapy water. Make a trial print with water on paper. Correct the block if necessary.

Printing. Squeeze the thick printing ink out of the tube on to the glass and spread it with a knife. See if it is the right consistency, and if necessary thin it with a few drops of turpentine (not substitute). Roll out the ink on the glass and coat the roller evenly. Then coat the block with the roller and make a trial print on paper by laying the paper on the block, rubbing the paper and pulling it off. Examine the print. Messy interspaces mean that ink is too thin; weak print, that either ink is too sparingly applied or too thick. After getting a satisfactory print on paper, print on the ironed fabric, laying the block down quickly without shifting it. Press it down evenly on the fabric with a rolling-pin or by laying a piece of wood on it and hammering on that. Or do the work on the floor and stand on the block. Then pull block and fabric apart quickly and evenly, either the block from the fabric or the other way round.

Finishing. Clean ink off block and other equipment with turpentine substitute. Leave printed fabric to dry. Wait four weeks before washing it.

You will need practice and experience to produce a lino cut as complicated as this. Prints of this kind were used at one time as trade marks on flour sacks

Stencilling

Another method of fabric printing is by the use of stencils. Choose a motif covering as much surface as possible and transfer it to stencilling card (waterproof card, oiled paper, lampshade card or varnished paper) and cut it out carefully with a sharp pair of scissors or a stencil knife.

You will then have two stencils, a positive and a negative one. The positive stencil consists of the rest of the card from which the motif has been cut out; the cut-out parts form the negative one. As a rule, especially if you are a beginner, you use the negative stencils, but more advanced printers can work with positive ones, or even with both kinds on the same piece of material. Pin the stencil firmly to the fabric and then pour a little fabric-painting ink into a saucer and dip the tip of a thick bristle paintbrush into it. Now paint all the edges of the stencil and all the spaces not covered by it. When the ink is dry, remove the stencil, and the motif will appear as a negative drawing in the colour of the fabric. If instead of the cut-out parts you use their frames, and paint the open spaces with ink, the motif will appear in the painted colour, and all the rest in the colour of the fabric which was covered up.

Equipment

As stencilling restricts you to patterns with large surfaces, coarse weaves such as linen mixtures are best, though other kinds may be used. In any case they must be free from dressing, and if you are not sure of this you must treat them like dressed fabrics and boil them in soapy water. If the fabric will not stand up to such a high temperature, wash it in warm soda water (one teaspoonful of soda to a quart of water). Synthetic-fibre fabrics and silk have no dressing in them.

Besides the fabric you will need stencil card, sold by stationers, or you can use oiled or varnished paper

31

Requirements for stencilling

. . . and pinned to the fabric

The rest of the fabric, not covered by the stencil, is painted with a short-haired brush dipped in the ink

or lampshade paper. If you have none of these handy, you can use ordinary card, painting the cut edges with oil colour to make them waterproof. You will also need a sharp-pointed pair of scissors or a stencil knife, a stout bristle paintbrush and fabric-painting ink.

Choice of motif
In the fabric-printing techniques earlier described, the nature of the block materials used (potatoes and linoleum) restricted the choice of motif. Stencilling allows more freedom, though this does not mean that you can run amok with colours and pattern design. Always remember that the success of the work depends on the harmony of colours and shapes. All that you learnt when printing from blocks—simplification and significant combination of forms, and limitation of colours—should be of the greatest use to you in designing stencils. Choose clear-cut ornament and stylised animal or plant forms rather than plastic representations of objects or human figures. Begin with simple things and elaborate by degrees.

Method of work
The motif, designed by yourself if possible, must be drawn on the stencil card, either freehand or traced over carbon paper, and cut out neatly with scissors or stencil knife. Avoid fine lines, because they will not cling to the fabric and are liable to break off. The stencil, which may consist of several parts, must be pinned to the fabric to form the complete pattern. Now pour some fabric-painting ink (permanent ink for light colours, permanent covering ink for dark fabrics) into a saucer and dip the tip of the bristle paintbrush into it, only taking up a little ink. If the brush is too full there is a risk of the ink seeping under the edges of the stencil and blurring the outlines. Begin by running the brush round

A stencilled pattern composed of seven combined parts appearing as a negative design in the colour of the fabric

the edges of the stencil, or the separate parts, holding them pressed down on the fabric as firmly as possible with your other hand. Then paint all the open spaces round them and let the ink dry thoroughly. Then remove the stencil, and the pattern will show up clearly on the fabric.

Uses for this method

Stencilled fabrics can be used for tablecloths and mats, cushion covers and curtains, scarves and kerchiefs and children's clothes. The choice of pattern should always depend on the proposed use, which should therefore have been settled before work is begun. In many cases the fabric can even be cut out before cutting the stencils, to make it easier to arrange the patterns. Paper as well as fabric can be decorated with stencilled patterns. Greeting cards treated in this way will bear a much more personal character than bought ones, however original.

Summary

Equipment. Coarse fabrics, free from dressing (linen mixtures), stencil card, fabric-painting inks, scissors or stencil knife, bristle paintbrush.

Preliminary work. Draw a bold, flat pattern and transfer it or draw it straight on the stencil card. Cut it out neatly. If you are not using the cut-out pieces but the card out of which they have been cut, you will have a positive stencil. You will then paint the holes, so to speak, and obtain a pattern from them, as below, and pin it to the fabric.

Method. Dip the paintbrush in a saucer filled with fabric-painting ink, taking only just enough on the tip of the brush. Press the stencil down firmly on the fabric, paint round the edges of the holes to begin with, and then fill in the holes. Allow the ink to dry and then remove the stencil.

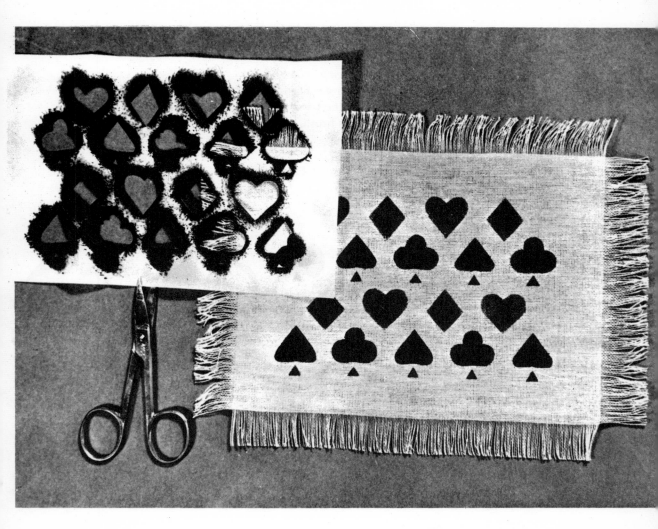

Here two methods were combined:
the full motifs were stencilled
and the figures on the watch
dials painted with a brush

Painting on fabric

To many people, painting on fabrics sounds incredibly old-fashioned. But the old sort of fabric painting, which was supposed in its day to imitate embroidery, has not the remotest connection with our subject.

Hardly any other method of textile decoration has such a variety of uses as fabric painting, which our grandmothers unfortunately brought into disrepute. The fabric-painting inks on the market today—except for a few inferior brands—have unlimited uses, since they are sun-proof and wash-proof, and will stand up to boiling and bad weather. They are therefore suitable for decorating children's clothes, curtains and wall coverings, as well as tablecloths, table mats, napkins and umbrellas. As the illustrations to this chapter show, attractive modern designs can be used. Of course not everybody is good at drawing. Those who find it difficult should begin with ornaments and very simple forms, with which quite pleasant effects can be obtained.

Tracing a pattern should always be regarded as a makeshift which will soon prove unsatisfying. Everybody should aim at producing their own designs.

Choice of fabric

Almost all smooth fabrics, free from dressing, are suitable, including linen, linen mixtures, cambric, silk, art silk, felt, wool and synthetic weaves; light and dark fabrics, coarse and fine, thick and thin, loose and close-woven. Those containing dressing must first be washed in hot soapy water, or better still, boiled. Otherwise you may ruin all your later work, since if you paint a fabric with dressing in it, the dye is not brought in immediate contact with the fibres but adheres only to the dressing, which is dissolved in the first wash, carrying the dye with it and leaving you with a washed-out, messy painting. There is also a risk that particles of dye set afloat in the water may cling to the fabric again and stain it.

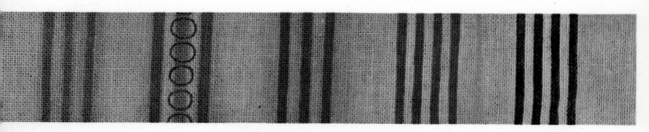

By way of practice,
begin with lines and simple
geometric forms

Equipment

Fabric painting requires very little equipment. You only need to have plenty of permanent inks in as many shades as possible, which can be mixed. Recently, permanent inks have been made available which will cover dark fabrics without allowing any of the ground colour to show through. White on black is now really white, and not grey as it used to be. All other shades show true to colour on a dark ground. This is a considerable advance, for up to now fabric painting on dark grounds was not very satisfactory. For light to medium-coloured fabrics take the usual permanent inks, and for all dark fabrics the new permanent covering inks. Besides the inks you will need one—or preferably several—good-quality hair paintbrushes.

Preliminary work

The fabric to be painted should be cut to the size required, because then the pattern can be more sensibly distributed. Table mats, napkins and other rectangular things must be cut along the threads. Design a simple, distinct pattern on a piece of paper (experts, of course, will draw straight on the fabric). If you cut the paper

This design, carried out on coarse
fabric, requires assured handling of
the paintbrush

just a little larger than the design you can try the effect more easily, by shifting it about. When you have found the best place for it, transfer the design to the fabric. On light-coloured fabrics this is done with black-lead paper, on dark ones with white-coated tracing paper. If you have none of this handy, rub some tailor's chalk over the back of your design and lay it on the fabric, white side down. Then draw the lines with some not-too-sharp implement, as though you were using tracing paper. The best way to go to work is to pin the design to the fabric, and then stretch this over a board (pastry board and drawing pins or thumb tacks). When you have transferred the design carefully, compare the original with the tracing on the fabric and make any completions or corrections that appear necessary.

Use of fabric-painting inks

If you want to use the inks as they come in the bottles, you can dip a clean paintbrush straight into the ink and begin painting, but the brush must only be inked about halfway up. More than that would be mere waste, because you do not paint with the upper half, and the ink would simply dry there. The metal part of the paintbrush must on no account come in contact with the ink.

To avoid mixing the inks, you must take a clean brush for each colour. This presents no difficulty if you have

Little equipment is needed for fabric painting

The fabric must be cut along the thread

The fabric must be the right size before beginning work

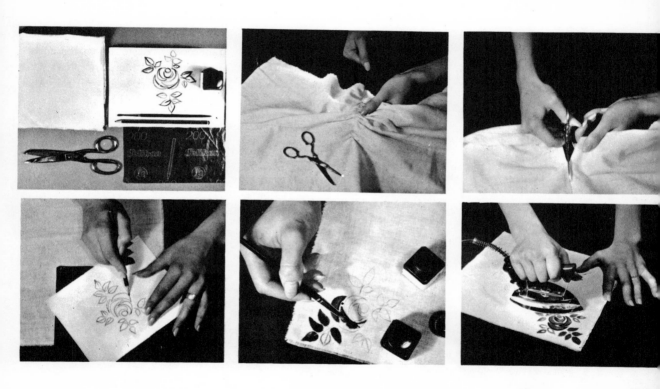

The pattern is traced through. (Later on you will draw straight on to the fabric)

The pattern is carefully painted

When dry, the painting is ironed on the wrong side

several brushes, otherwise the brush must be thoroughly washed out in clean water at the end of each operation with any one colour. It is unwise to use any sort of chemical cleaner for the purpose, because the chemical composition of the different inks is often unknown. If several colours are to be mixed, pour a little of each colour into a neutral vessel. Try to mix the right amount at the start. If there is too little of it, it is nearly always difficult to produce the same shade in a fresh mixture. If there is too

much—the lesser evil—it means an unnecessary waste of material, because the mixed inks do not keep. This is especially the case with inks that have been mixed with white.

Painting the pattern

When painting the pattern on the fabric you should always have a scrap of the same material beside you, either for testing the effect of the colour, or merely for wiping the paintbrush on it. Begin painting with the lightest

Simple patterns on coarse fabric are specially effective

PUNCH AND JUDY SHOW

When painting on fabric it is not necessary to complete the outlines of the pattern with a stroke of the brush, as was done on p. 39

colour and end with the darkest. As far as the position of the colours allows, begin in the upper left-hand corner, and work so as to end up, as nearly as possible, in the lower right-hand corner (as when writing). In this way you will avoid resting your hand on the painted surface and blurring it. Do not start on a fresh colour until the one before is dry, otherwise they may run into each other somewhere.

However, as fabric-painting inks dry very quickly, work can proceed, on the whole, at a good pace.

It is advisable to stretch thin fabrics before painting them, so that they lie free. You can do this by slipping a piece of wood or a strip of cardboard right and left between the underlay and the fabric. This will prevent the superfluous ink, not absorbed by the fabric, and dripping through, from accumulating on the underlay and smearing the fabric. This precaution is not necessary with coarse weaves.

Finishing

When all the painting has been done and the ink is dry, iron the fabric on the wrong side with as hot an iron as possible. The dye will then be absolutely ingrained in the fabric. With synthetic fibres like nylon, perlon, etc., which must not be ironed hot, the painting will only prove fast if washed in the mild solutions generally used for such fabrics. All other fabrics can be washed and boiled without injuring the painting, provided no inferior inks have been used.

Summary

For the day when you can make use of all you have learnt in your first attempts, here are the essential points once more in brief:

Uses. Children's clothes, aprons, table-cloths, napkins, table mats, towels, laundry bags, curtains, wall hangings, kerchiefs, scarves, gloves and umbrellas.

Fabrics. Smooth fabrics free from dressing, in cotton, silk, art silk, cambric, linen, linen mixtures, felt and synthetic materials.

Inks. Permanent inks for light to medium-dark fabrics. Permanent covering inks for dark fabrics.

Pattern. Simple, covering large areas, few details, gay in colour but not garish.

Method. Draw the pattern on paper and transfer it by tracing. Test it, and if necessary correct or complete it on the fabric. Then paint it in with the brush. Dip only clean brushes into the ink. For mixing, use a neutral vessel. Start painting at the top left-hand corner and work towards the lower right-hand corner. Lightest colours first, darkest last.

Fixing. Iron fabric with hot iron on wrong side (synthetic fabrics only at the permitted temperature).

Batik

Batik is one of the most beautiful hand fabric-printing techniques. This ancient folk art is ascribed to the Javanese, but its origin is not really known for certain. Batik is a method of dyeing, the effect of which is obtained by an interplay of spaces and colours. Even as children many of us without realising it became acquainted with a kind of batik. When Easter eggs were dyed, and first had tapes or threads tied round them, or grass glued on them before being laid in the dye bath, they absorbed the dye only in the vacant spaces, and the covered parts came out white when the eggs were unwrapped.

This is exactly what happens in the genuine batik technique. Melted wax is spread here and there on the fabric, which is then immersed in the prepared dye bath and dyed in all the places not covered by the wax. Batik work is recognisable, above all, by the typical crackles or veins caused by the cracking of the wax and the penetration of the dye where this occurs.

Equipment

All light-coloured fabrics are suitable, provided they are free from dressing and will stand up to a temperature of at least 130° Fahrenheit. Fabrics with dressing in them must be boiled in soapy water or washed in hot soda water before dyeing, otherwise paricles of dye would be carried away with the dressing and the whole pattern would become blurred. The most suitable fabrics are thin ones like silk, art silk, voile and cambric. The heavier and coarser the fabric the more dye it will absorb. You must, therefore, not only have enough dye available, but the dye bath itself must be large enough. Besides which, coarse, heavy fabrics dry more slowly than thin fabrics, so that the dyeing operation will take proportionately more time, especially if several colours are used. The wax penetrates the thicker fabrics more slowly too, so that you may have to paint a fresh coat of wax on the wrong side.

Batik tools and accessories can be

bought as sets in boxes. They are more expensive than if bought separately, but it is handy to have everything together. A beginner, therefore, is well advised to buy a box by way of basic equipment. In time he will need more batik wax and many more different dyes, and this supplementary equipment can then be bought bit by bit.

Besides the fabric, you will need the following: batik wax, a spirit lamp (or source of gentle heat), a wooden frame (knock one up out of four strips, or take a tray or an old picture frame), large and small paintbrushes, preferably bristle, for coating the spaces, and a little wax can (oil can) for drawing the finer lines. But above all you must have the right fabric dyes. They must be dyes that can be used cold— or, rather, lukewarm. Most dyeing methods require boiling hot solutions, so you must not use these. Before starting work, have a container ready —a clean tin will do—for melting the wax, a vessel (not metal) for stirring the dye, and a cloth (preferably perlon or nylon) for straining it.

Choice of pattern
In artistic work such as hand fabric decoration one should never be too ambitious. What is the use of launching out on a complicated piece of work that is bound to be an obvious failure? You get no pleasure out of it yourself, and the most other people can do is to praise it out of politeness or pity. Above all, a job that has misfired is likely to discourage you from persevering before you have really begun. You had far better work out a simple pattern as well as possible. The old saying 'slow and sure' holds good here. Begin by trying to 'think in reverse', as though your design were a photographic negative. For instance, you may want to make a blue cloth with a white snowman on it. Take a piece of white paper the size of your fabric and draw the outline of the snowman on it, with his

Batik design on silk in soft pastel
colours, produced by three successive
dyeings

hat, his broom and all the other details. Now imagine how he will turn out later on, when you have covered him with wax on the fabric. He will remain white like the fabric itself. But what about the details—the buttons, the nose, the face? You will have to keep the fabric free of wax in those places.

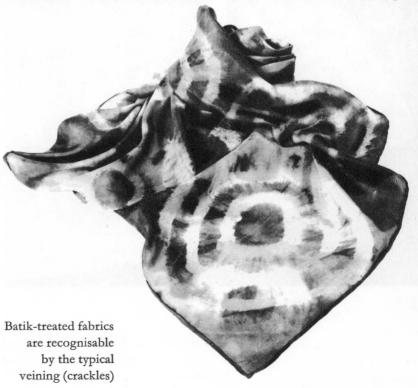

Batik-treated fabrics
are recognisable
by the typical
veining (crackles)

Make a couple of drawings and try to imagine the finished batik, keeping, as I have said, to quite simple shapes, and avoiding 'jumpy' work, which will be all the more difficult to see as a whole when it is complicated later on by the crackles. Lively batik is only effective when it is produced by design and with the requisite skill. And this skill can only be acquired step by step, beginning with simple attempts.

Transfer of the drawing

If you are using thin fabrics—and beginners should always do so—there is no difficulty in working from a drawing of the pattern. It must first be gone over in Indian ink, drawing the outlines very heavily, so that the paper need only be slipped under the fabric and the pattern will show through clearly enough.

You can then draw the pattern on the fabric with a soft pencil, keeping the coloured sketch beside you. *Later on* you will work mostly free-hand. If the fabric is so thick that you cannot see the drawing through it, the drawing must be transferred to the fabric with the help of black-lead paper (not carbon paper). You can make this by scribbling with a soft pencil on the back of tracing paper or thin drawing paper, and spreading the graphite over the surface. Black-lead paper will leave light grey lines on the fabric, which will be enough to work by.

If you have none of this paper handy, or cannot obtain it, there is another way which, though rather complicated, will serve in an emergency.

The drawing must be gone over with a hard pencil, heavily enough to make the lines stand out on the back of the paper. They are then redrawn with a very blunt, soft pencil so that the pattern shows on both sides of the paper. If you then lay the drawing right side up (with the redrawn side against the fabric) you need only go over all the lines again. The soft pencil marks on the back will come off on the fabric clearly enough for you to work from them without difficulty.

Working with batik wax

Now the wooden frame mentioned at the beginning comes into action. The fabric is stretched over it with drawing pins or thumb tacks, so that when it is coated with wax it will not stick to the surface beneath it (table or whatever). If you have no frame, you can manage another way. Stretch the fabric, not too tightly, over a wooden board on two sides only, leaving the top and bottom edges open. Then slip a little strip of wood right and left between board and fabric, so that the fabric lies free and the wax cannot stick to the board.

Meanwhile the wax must be heated (over a spirit lamp or a plate-warmer) till it is fluid, so that you can paint with it. You can then put it on with either a paintbrush or the little oil can. The paintbrush is used for coating the large areas, while the little oil can is indispensable for drawing the fine lines. It is used as follows: batik wax is grated on a kitchen grater and poured into the can through the large opening, then the can is held slantwise over the spirit lamp so that as the wax melts it will not run out of the hair-fine spout. It is only held in the normal position when drawing on the fabric. You must work very rapidly because the wax soon cools, though of course it can always be reheated.

When doing this, you can resort to a little trick. First heat the wax in the body of the can till it has melted, and only then the wax in the spout. As long as the spout is choked with the cold wax it will hold back the wax in the can.

If the fabric is so thick that the wax has not penetrated everywhere to the wrong side, it must be coated with wax again on the right side. The hotter and more fluid the wax, the more easily it will penetrate the fabric.

Equipment required
for batik

The fabric is stretched over a frame

Painting on the wax. The pattern
drawing is under the fabric

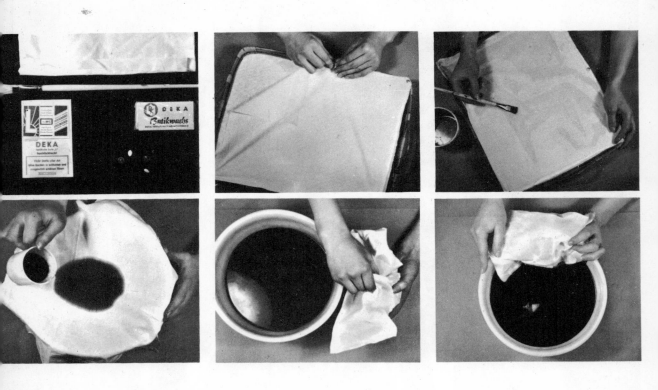

. . . and strained through
a cloth into a bowl

The fabric with the wax on it is dipped
in cold water and crumpled before
dyeing, so that the wax will break here
and there

The fabric is laid loosely in the dye
bath

Hot water is poured on the dye . . .

The dyed and dried fabric is ironed hot between sheets of newspaper—which must be constantly changed—to melt the wax and thus remove it

At your first attempt you should, of course, aim at a two-colour batik, i.e. only one dyeing operation. In this case all you need remember, when painting on the wax, is that everything covered by it will remain light, while the free areas on the fabric will take up the dye. When using the wax, unforeseen alterations may occur in the pattern owing to splashes or to faulty drawing; but this doesn't matter. On the contrary, it may even lend the work the particular charm that only hand-made things can possess.

Preparing the dye bath
While the wax coating is drying, the dye bath is prepared. Pour boiling water into a little vessel, which must not be metal, and dissolve the dye powder in it. Then another vessel (again, not metal) must be prepared for the dyeing. It must be large enough for the fabric to float loosely in it. Stir the dye and pour it into the

dye bath through a piece of non-fraying material (perlon or nylon), adding hot water containing one tablespoonful of cooking salt to every four ounces of fabric. The dye bath must be hot, but it must not exceed a temperature of 130° Fahrenheit, otherwise the wax coating will melt.

Dyeing

To enable the fabric to absorb the dye evenly when it is laid in the dye bath, it should first be dipped in cold water, and more or less crumpled—according to taste. This makes the wax break here and there and let the dye through, producing the typical crackles (veins, marblings). The fabric is then laid loosely in the dye bath, using two pieces of wood free from splinters (wooden spoon handles or the like), or else putting on rubber gloves. The fabric must be continually stirred in the bath to make it absorb the dye evenly. The dyeing will take from 15 to 30 minutes, according to the shade required. The deeper the colour is to be, the longer the fabric must be left in the bath, bearing in mind that it will look several shades darker while it is wet. But the depth of the colour depends not only on the length of the operation but on the temperature of the dye bath (the cooler the bath, the weaker the colour) and on the quantity of dye powder used.

The greatest depth of colour is reached in 30 minutes. Allow the fabric to drip (never wring it) and rinse it in cold water till the water runs clear. Then hang it up to dry. It must not be thrown over a line. The best way is to peg it loosely to the line with plastic pegs, in the open air. If the drying takes too long it can be hastened a little with a hair drier, but this must on on account be set at 'hot'.

The characteristic crackles
give batik work a very
lively effect; they should
therefore not be made too
bright. This silk scarf
is in grey, black and orange
on a white ground.
Its skilful spacing gives
it a restful and harmonious
effect

55

Finishing

When the fabric is dry the wax must be removed. This is the most exciting part of the work, because now one can see how it has turned out. To remove the wax, lay the fabric between several sheets of newspaper and run a hot iron to and fro over it till the wax melts and runs into the paper. The paper will have to be constantly changed so that it can absorb all the wax. Do not use the latest newspapers, lest the fresh printing ink come off on the fabric. It is all right to see things on batik, but not to read them.

If large areas have been coated with wax, the fabric can be laid in benzine or benzol to remove it more rapidly, but as both of these are highly inflammable, it is best to use them in the open, and of course not near a naked light.

When the wax has been removed the work is at an end, and if you have followed instructions and done the work carefully, your batik should be a success.

Summary

Uses of batik. Batik-treated fabrics are minor treasures, whose special value consists in their uniqueness, since it is hardly possible to produce two exactly alike. They are specially suitable for scarves, kerchiefs and shoulder wraps, and for ornamental silk ribbons. But these beautiful fabrics can also be designed as wall hangings, cushion covers and even blouses.

Equipment. Batik wax and dyes, paintbrush, little oil can for the wax, spirit lamp, dressing-free fabric, stretching frame or board, tin.

Draw pattern on paper (or straight on the fabric), possibly also a model in Indian ink.

Coat the areas and lines to be left blank with hot, liquid wax. For coating with the paintbrush, melt the wax in a tin; for coating with the little can, fill it with grated wax and heat it over the spirit lamp.

The dye bath. Put dye in a small vessel (not of metal) and pour boiling water on it. Then pour it through a non-fraying cloth into a larger vessel filled with enough lukewarm water (this vessel also must not be metal). Maximum temperature 130°F. Do not forget the cooking salt—one table-spoon to every four ounces of fabric. *Crackles* are produced by crumpling the fabric after dipping it in cold water.

Time for dyeing. From 15 to 30 minutes according to depth of colour. Wet fabric looks darker. Do not take it out of the dye bath too soon.

Rinsing and drying. After dyeing, rinse the fabric in cold water till the water runs clear. Let the fabric drip. Do not wring it, or throw it over the line to dry, but fasten it up loosely with plastic pegs.

Remove wax by ironing with hot iron between sheets of old newspaper (constantly changed) or blotting-paper. If necessary, remove large areas of wax by laying the fabric in benzine or benzole, working out of doors, as both are inflammable. Use a glass, china or enamel vessel, not a metal one.

Multi-coloured batik

In this case the fabric is immersed in different dye baths, with fresh wax treatment between, working gradually from the lightest colours to the darkest. For example, if you want to print a yellow cock with a red comb and black tail feathers on a white ground, you proceed as follows. First, everything that is to be left white is coated with wax, then the whole fabric can be dyed yellow. After rinsing and drying in the open air, everything that is to be left yellow (in this case the whole body of the cock) must be coated with wax, without removing any of the first coating. The areas now left free must be dyed bright red, and then rinsed and dried. Finally, coat everything that is to stay red with wax, and immerse in the last, black dye bath. For the final treatment, proceed as before (rinsing, drying, removing wax). In this instance, owing to a suitable choice of colours, it was possible to dye the colours one over another (red on yellow, black on red), because each of them was covered by the next, darker one. But the red will have tended towards orange, and the black towards brown. Avoid disappointment by allowing for these modifications when settling your colour scheme.

You can of course proceed in another way, by using dye remover between each operation. That is to say, in the case of the cock, all the yellow parts to be dyed red must first be treated with the remover, and later all the red parts that are to be dyed black. But this method is not recommended. In the original batik technique each colour is obtained by using a different dye bath, and every part of the fabric that is not to be of this colour must therefore be coated with wax, so that you have a perpetual succession of coating, dyeing, drying, coating,

dyeing, and so on, till the fabric has acquired all the desired colours. A very complicated process and, for beginners, a very confusing one.

Do not be lured into playing about with too many colours, under the impression that you are being 'modern'. Even a multi-coloured batik should not undergo more than three dyeings, especially as you can produce innumerable shades by dyeing one colour over another.

Imitation batik

This technique is barred by professionals as unorthodox. Fundamentally, however, it differs very little from that already described. The fabric is coated in places with batik wax, and the remainder dyed, but not immersed in a dye bath for each colour. The areas between the waxed lines and patches are painted in with a paintbrush. The powder dyes in the chosen colours are shaken into different little vessels (not metal) and boiling water is poured over them, the painting being then done with these colour concentrates. When the work has reached the stage of being rinsed clear and dried, the areas painted in colour are coated with wax, keeping carefully to the outlines, and the final dyeing (largest areas, darkest colour) is done in a dye bath in the usual way. Finishing is carried out in the same way as with all other ordinary batik methods.

But it must not be forgotten that batik produced in this way is not wash-proof. Painting the dye on the fabric tends to oversaturate the fibres, i.e. they get more dye than they can absorb, and they get rid of this again in the wash, so that in time the colour becomes increasingly paler, and the different colours run into one another. Besides which, in imitation batik the dye is used cold, and cannot therefore combine so thoroughly with the fabric.

Imitation batik, which can be given many more forms than true batik, is a useful form of practice for beginners, but it differs essentially from true batik and other associated techniques by the absence of crackles.

Tied batik

This is a technique that has really nothing in common with batik except the name. 'Batik', translated, means something like 'writing' or 'painting', and in tied batik nothing of this sort is done.

A light fabric, free from dressing, is tied up here and there with silk threads into little lumps like warts. The fabric is then immersed in a dye bath prepared in the usual way, thoroughly rinsed and hung up to dry. The silk threads are then untied and the fabric is ironed out. The places that were tied up will have remained uncoloured, and the result is a scatter pattern of clustered rays. These tied batiks can be very attractive, and they are specially suitable for tablecloths, napkins, kerchiefs and scarves.